Can You Find, Did You Know Series

Copyright ©2022 by
Quintina Publishing, LLC & CJ Corki

All Rights Reserved. No part of this book may be used or reproduced in any way without written permission except in the case except in the case of brief quotations embodied in critical articles or reviews.

Thank you for buying an authorized edition of this book and for complying with copyright laws by not reproducing, scanning, or distributing any part of it in any form without permission. You are supporting writers and their hard work by doing this.

For information contact:
Quintina Publishing LLC @ https://www.cjcorki.com or
CJ Corki at: author@cjcorki.com

ISBN Paperback: 978-0-9980393-9-8

Library of Congress Cataloging-in-Publication-Data is available
Printed in the United States of America

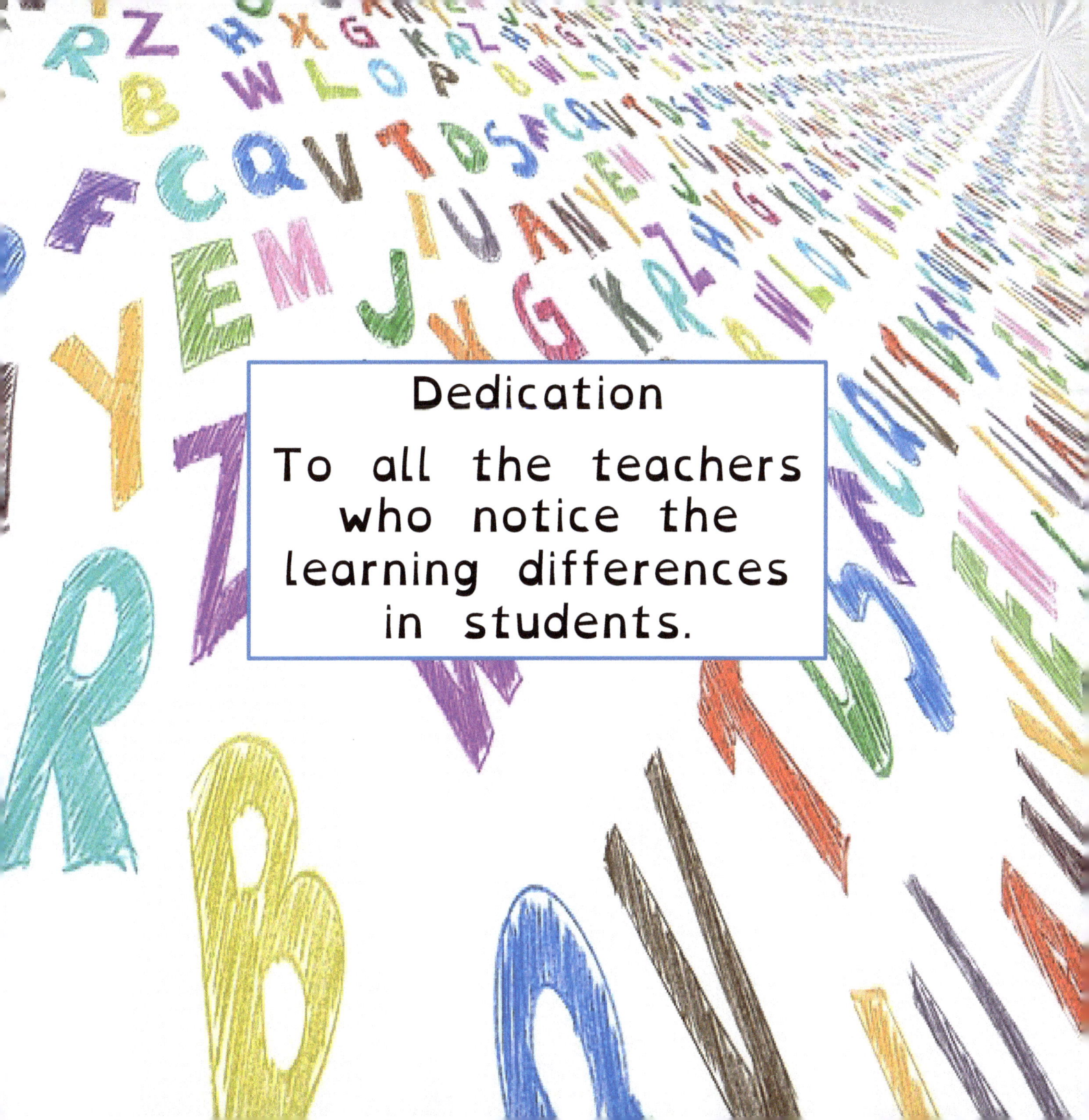

Dedication

To all the teachers who notice the learning differences in students.

Practicing Words with S'more's ABCs

by CJ Corki

Before the Marshmallows became a Mystery

Can You Find, Did You Know Series

Do, Find, Know

Let's make learning letters and words fun!

The first step is to check out the pictures. Grab a pencil and trace the letters on each of the pages. Each page has one letter of the alphabet.

Then, Let's Play Bingo! Look at the pictures on the bingo card and see how many you can find. Don't forget to check them off after you find them. There are hints on where to look for them on the Can You Find pages.

In addition, there is a **Did You Know** section to learn something new about the alphabet items in the book.

Have fun!

CJ Corki

A a

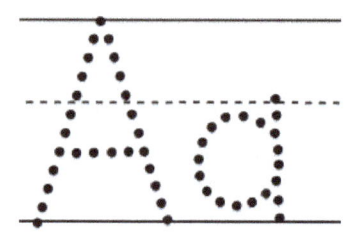

ant

bird

Bb

cat

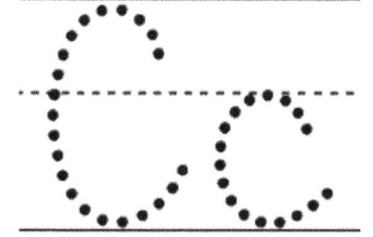 

Dd

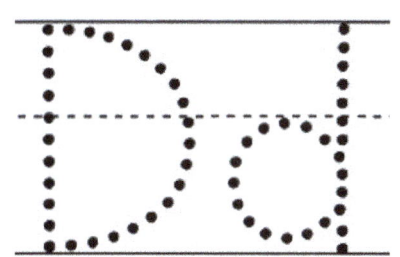

dog

Ee

Ee

egg

flag

F f

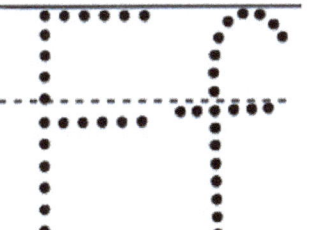

Hh

hat

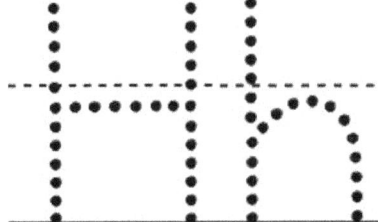

I i

ice

jar

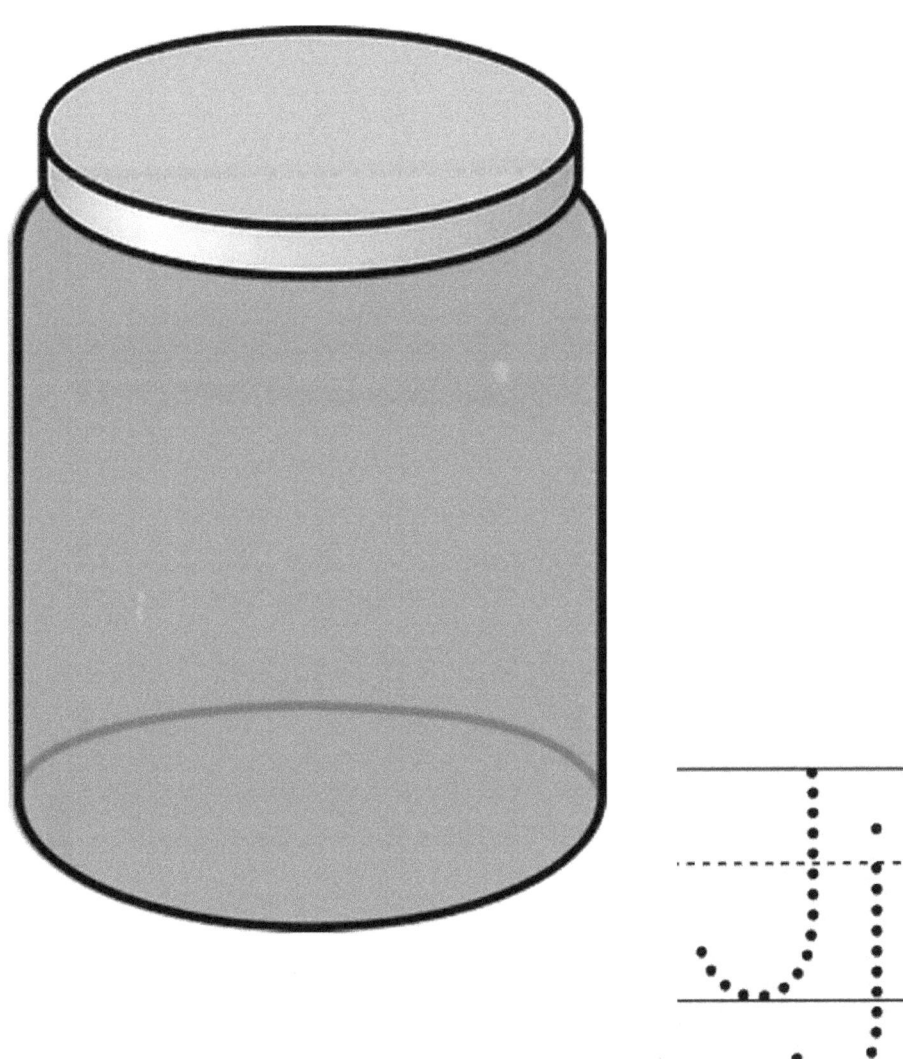

Jj

key

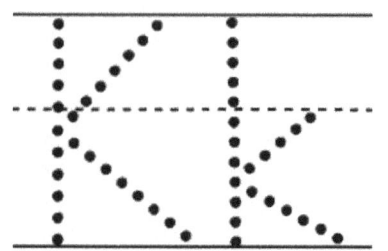

Kk

Ll

Lip

Mm

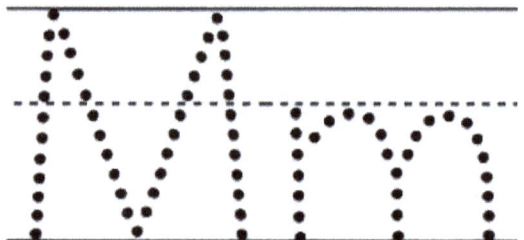

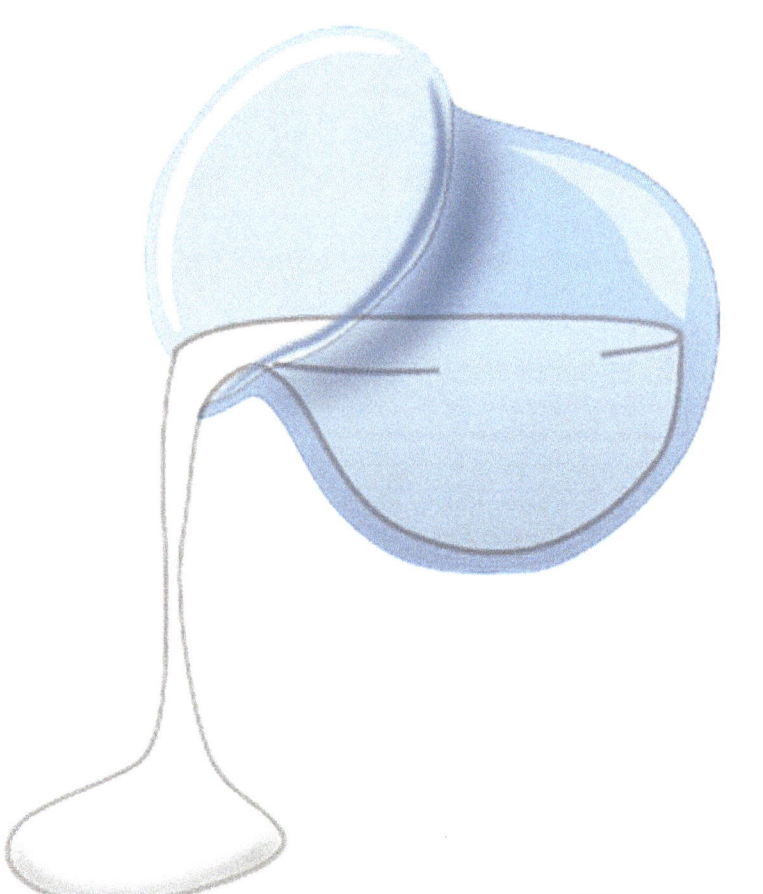

milk

nest

Nn

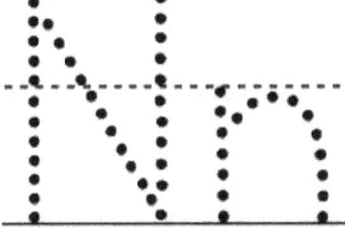

owl

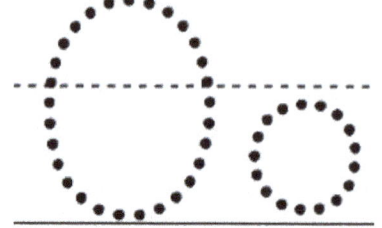 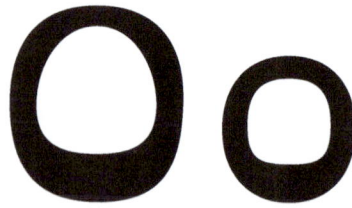

Pp Pp

pump

Q q

quilt

rock

R r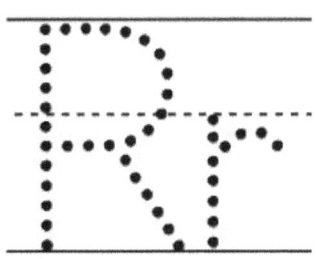

swing

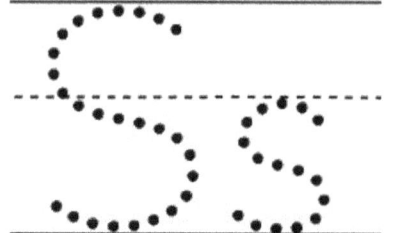 Ss

Tt

toad

Uu

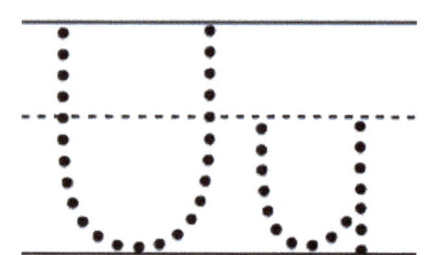

cUp

van

Vv

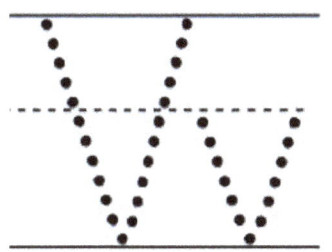

well

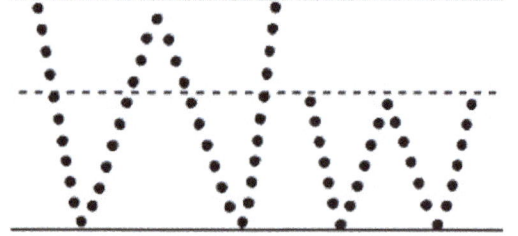

W w

X x

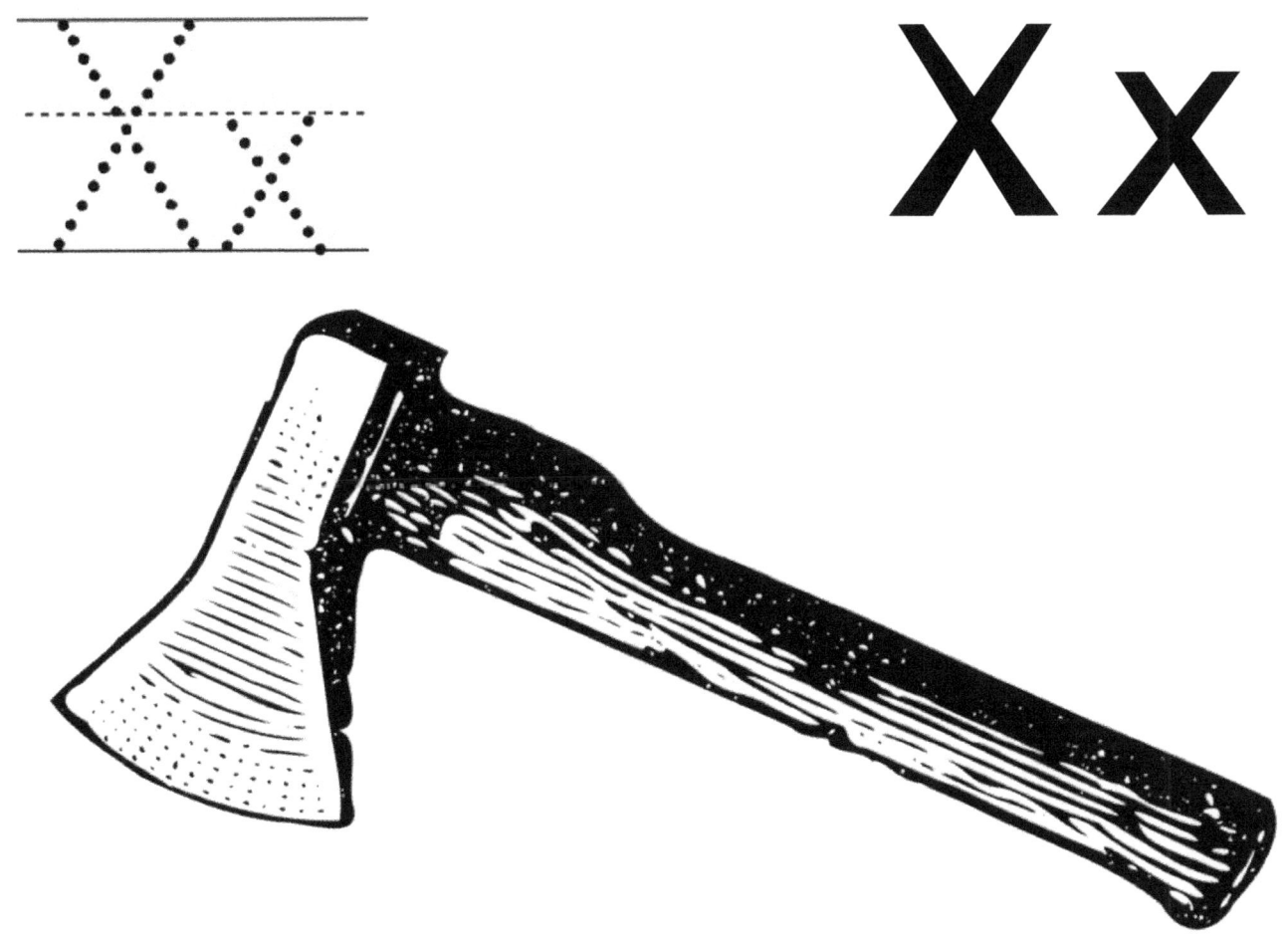

aXe

Yy

yarn

ZOO

Z z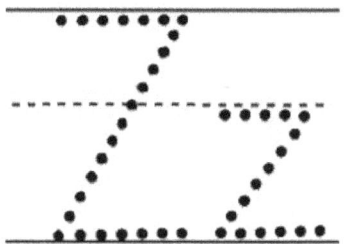

THE MARSHMALLOW MYSTERY
Bingo

Can You Find?

Can you find these in YOUR community? Cross off each one when you find it until you win Bingo.

Can You Find?

Ant – look on the ground or under a rock. Spring and fall is the easiest time to find them.

Bird – like to perch, which means sit on a branch, or tree limb or wires. Don't forget to listen and you will hear them sing. Chickens are also birds.

Cat – like a dog are typically pets. If you don't have one in your house. Check with neighbors and friends.

Can You Find?

Dog — typically a family pet. If you don't have one check with neighbors and friends. Don't approach unless you get permission first.

Egg — look in your refrigerator. They are always refrigerated, unless you go to a farm.

Flag — flags can be found in many places, your home, on TV during a sports event or at government buildings.

Can You Find?

Girl — this could be you, or someone else in your house. Remember moms and grandmas are girls too.

Hat — there are lots of different types of hats, baseball caps count too.

Ice — open your freezer and you will easily find ice.

Can You Find?

Jar — Look in the pantry, jars are made of glass, and they hold yummy food like peanut butter, honey, tomato sauce, and so much more.

Key — Find it on a chair or on a ring. Used to lock and unlock things.

Lip — Look in the mirror, faces have them and depending how you shape them will show people how you are feeling. The best shape for lips is a smile.

Can You Find?

Milk — When you visit a farm, look for cows, sheep, goats, and other animals, they all give us milk. The milk in your refrigerator can be put on your cereal.

Nest — Go to your yard or nearest park and find a nest up in the trees but don't climb the tree or touch the nest.

Owl — Look up in the trees and if you can see one you might hear them at night with a hoot-hoot or maybe a loud screech.

Can You Find?

Pump — Put your hand over your heart and feel it beat, your heart is a *pump* too.

Quilt — Made of patches of fabric, sewn together to make a cozy blanket. Is there one on your bed?

Rock — Look on the ground and you will find them, most are hard, but some are soft. Find one by a lake, throw it hard and skip it on the water.

Can You Find?

Swing - Look at a playground. It could be a tire swing, baby swing, or porch swing.

Toad - Look for toads in yards, and gardens during the summer. Don't catch it. Let it be free.

c**Up** – Look in your kitchen in the morning. Does any adult in your house drink coffee? Or do you have hot chocolate? Or a tea party?

Can You Find?

Van – Do your parents drive a van? What about friends or neighbors? Look on the roads when your parents are driving.

Well - You can find a well on a farm, or maybe a decorative wishing wells in their yard. A wishing well is when you throw a penny into the well and make a wish.

aXe- An axe is heavy and sharp. You might find an axe in a garage, or barn or home improvement stores. Don't touch the axe without a grown up.

Can You Find?

Yarn - The easiest way to find yarn is to find a sweater. Someone knitted the sweater from yarn.

Zoo — A trip to the zoo is always fun to see lions and tigers and bears, but sometimes it isn't possible. Find a zoo animal amongst your stuffed animals.

Did You Know?

Did you Know?

Ant – Ants are ridiculously strong. They can carry between 10 and 50 times their own body weight!

Bird - Chickens and ostriches are thought to be descendants of the Tyrannosaurus rex.

Cats - Cats are supposed to have 18 toes (five toes on each front paw; four toes on each back paw).

Dog - When dogs kick backward after they go to the bathroom it's not to cover it up, but to mark their territory, using the scent glands in their feet.

Egg – the average American eats around 286 eggs a year.

Did you Know?

Flag – 5 American flags have been to the moon.

Girl – have a heightened sense of smell. They helped our ancestors survive since women were mainly gatherers, helped them to pick the right foods for the family.

Hat - The colors of hard hats have specific meanings. White hard hats are worn by engineers, green by safety inspectors, yellow by laborers, and orange or pink hard hats are used by a visitor.

Ice – is a common name for frozen water. Liquid water freezes and becomes ice at 32 degrees Fahrenheit.

Jar – A Mason jar is a glass jar with a screw-on cap or wire-sprung lid.

Did you Know?

Key - The locks and keys used in the early Egyptian dynasties were made of wood. The Ancient Greeks were the first to create keys out of metal.

Lip – "My lips are sealed" used to say that you will not repeat somebody's secret to other people.

Milk - In addition to cows, the following animals provide milk for dairy products: Sheep, goats, horses and donkeys.

Nest - Nests are built by birds, but also mammals, fish, insects and reptiles.

Owl - Unlike most birds, owls make virtually no noise when they fly. Their soft down feathers muffle noise.

Did you Know?

Pump - A device used to move liquids or gases around. Your heart is a pump too. It moves your blood around.

Quilt - Some quilts are not used as bed covering but hung on a wall or otherwise displayed.

Rock - A geologic substance composed of minerals.

Swing - Swinging can help children maintain focus and attention even after they are off the swings. Just a few minutes on a swing can carry on into the classroom, improving a child's ability to concentrate.

Toad - Toads may play dead or puff themselves up to appear bigger if they feel threatened by predators. A group of toads is often called a knot.

cUp – Early mugs date back to the Stone Age and were made from bone and had no handles.

Did you Know?

Van- Van is short for "caravan." The first record of the term was introduced in 1829 to define a 'covered wagon.'

Well - Wells started Roman times because of the springs that bubble up there. Its name is from these springs which can today be found in the gardens.

aXe - Axes are simple machines. Axes are usually made of some sort of metal with a wooden handle. They are in the category of wedges. They are usually made of some sort of metal, mainly steel or iron. Don't touch an axe without a grown-up present.

Yarn - The earliest known samples of fabrics and yarns were found in Switzerland and were thought to be nearly 7,000 years old!

Zoo - The USA has at least 355 zoos. Philadelphia Zoo opened on July 1st, 1874 and is the oldest zoo in the USA.

Did you Know about Dyslexia?

One in five children have dyslexia. It can be identified as early as 3 years old. Early identification is key. Know the signs.

Preschool

- Has a hard time learning nursery rhymes or song lyrics that rhyme

- Speech delays...talking like a younger child

- Calling things by the wrong name...or hard time coming up with the name a simple objects

- Has trouble remembering things in the right order, like singing the letters of the alphabet or following directions.

Grade School

- Has trouble sounding out words

- Confused or board with books...not remembering the details of a story.

- Often confuses letters that look similar (b, d, p, q) and letters with similar sounds (d/t; b/p; f/v)

- Has trouble with spelling

- Often doesn't recognize common words

- Difficulty taking notes from the board

- Is confused with idioms...RAIN or SHINE

About the Authors

CJ Corki is a pen name tribute to the father of three of five sisters. CJ represents his initials, and Corki is Polish derivative of daughters; thus, CJ's daughters. These women dealt with the challenges of balancing work, life, and reluctant readers by day developing into amateur children's book sleuths by night... while wearing their bunny slippers, of course.

At an early age they learned to "play nice in the sandbox" and they hope to inspire others to remember the value of family, the importance of individual abilities, and to work together in harmony.

They currently live in different states but figured out how to stay close through video chat, phone calls, countless texts and their love for words. They adore their grand babies and they're busy living out their happily ever afters with their respective fur-babies and supportive husbands.

www.ingramcontent.com/pod-product-compliance
Lightning Source LLC
Chambersburg PA
CBHW061155010526
44118CB00027B/2977